#IStillBelieve:
We Have the Victory!

Asia Thomas

Copyright © 2017 Asia Thomas

All rights reserved.

ISBN:0692974385

ISBN-13:978-0692974384

Asia Thomas

TABLE OF CONTENTS

Dedication

Acknowledgements

Foreword

Preface

Chapter 1- #IStillBelieve

Chapter 2- #FaithOverGreif

Chapter 3- #FaithOverFlesh

Chapter 4- #FaithOverFear

Chapter 5- #FaithOverRejection

Chapter 6- #FaithOverFailure

Chapter 7- #Victory

#Dedication

I dedicate this book to my mom, Lynette White. #IStillBelieve: We have the Victory, is for us. I have seen you go through so much but your name is Victory! I look forward to all God is going to do through you and our family. Our faith shall make us whole!

To my older sister, Ashley Stephens, and her five children Ja'Darian, Trinity, Dream, Serenity and Destin.

Destin: You are destined for greatness. You are strong. You are smart. You are beautiful and caring. You are an overcomer and although you never got to know your mom, she loved you very much. She is a part of you and she lives on in you. People wanted to name you Destiny but she stood firm that your name was going to be Destin. I believe it's because she knew the meaning of your name.

Destin- to set apart for a particular use, purpose, design; intend. to appoint or ordain beforehand, as by divine decree; foreordain; predetermine.

God is going to use your life mightily! I can never replace your mother but I will always be here for you!

Ja' darian: You are the oldest. You paved the way for the others. Your mother captured every moment with you. She was so proud to call you son. You showed her unconditional love and she loved you unconditionally. You are smart, caring, kind, and handsome ☺. There is nothing you can't do, be or achieve. Continue to seek God and put Him first. You are a Kingdom Kid!

Trinity: You are the first baby girl. A daughter your mother sought to really bond with and teach all the things she knew so you never made the same mistakes she did. She wanted to protect you. She loved you and you made her proud to be a mom. You look just like her, you talk like her and even do some of the same things she did. You're special, beautiful and you possess the heart of God. Never allow anyone to change or influence you outside of who you are and what you know. Jesus lives in you girl! You are different. You are special. Be all He has called you to be Trinity!

Dream: You're such a smart and brilliant young boy. You are a natural leader. You mother loved you and was so proud of you. You made her happy. Your random hugs and kisses gave her life meaning. Live to your fullest potential. You're gifted. Never forget who the gifts and talents come from. Let Christ be seen in everything you do! Don't follow the crowd. You are destined to lead. Lead righteously. Nothing is impossible for you. Jesus lives in you!

Serenity: I think your mother was really looking for peace when you were born. You gave that to her. You brought so much joy to her life and your smile lit up the room. You are a gift from God, a gift your mother was happy to have. Serenity never lose your peace, your joy, your smile, your ability to let things go, your friendliness and love for people. You are special. You are important. You are valuable. God has great things in store for you!

#Acknowledgements

My Lord and Savior Jesus Christ. You give me the faith to believe. Thank you for being forever faithful even when I was Faith-Less. Everything I do and everything I am belongs to you.

My Pastors: Yaquis Shelley and Cameika Shelley, you have been the tangible example of what faith looks like. Thanks for believing in the God in me. Thanks for creating an environment that supports, corrects and challenges me to reach my fullest potential. I love my church THOTL! I am who I am because of you.

My mom, Lynnette White, you instilled faith in me at a tender age and for that I'm forever thankful. I love you.

My dad, James Thomas, I love you. Thanks for

always making sure I have had everything I need.

My grandmother, Jannie Hitchcock, thanks for always being there. I love you.

My sister, my best friend, April Franklin, I'm so proud of the woman of God you have become. I love you always. To my brother-in law, Quaris Franklin, you and April are testaments of what God can do!

To my nephews, Gabriel and Zion, future men of valor, men of prayer, men of faith, men of God. I love y'all so much!

To my family and friends, too many to name. Each of you have played a special part in my life. I love y'all!

To all those who have helped and supported with the process and outcome of this book, I am thankful!

#Foreword

God is completing through people what He has begun. Philippians 1:6 declares, "Being confident of this very thing, that He which hath begun a good work in you will perform it until the day of Jesus Christ." We see that the phrase, "Day of Christ" refers to a promise for believers in Him. Which is far different than the phrase, "Day of the Lord"; which is directed towards unbelievers. "Day of Christ" is basically for the Church (the Body of Christ) a day of blessings and reward, a heavenly hope, and an eagerly anticipated promise. In other words, the Apostle Paul writes to the church in Philippians to be confident that God who has started an amazing good work in you will perform or make it come to pass until it's time for you to be rewarded for your labor. That's what comes to mind when I read "I Still Believe."

As Senior Pastor of The Hand of the Lord

International Church for over 16 years and having been in ministry all together over 23 years, I have had the opportunity to see the hand of God in many ways. The most lasting is in the lives of His people. A little over 8 years ago I had the opportunity to witness His handy work at work in the life of one Asia Thomas.

I remember meeting the rebellious, self-centered, young lady walking in her own righteousness. The same young lady who would pen this masterpiece of an assignment. She wasn't who we know her to be today, she was very, very different. Nothing about her then would have read what you see today. But God! I've seen God over the years take an unlikely candidate and bring forth an amazing treasure. "I Still Believe," will take you on a life changing journey filled with real life accounts of a person's life as God was and is still completing what He has begun. You will leave with restored hope and faith in the plan of God. You will find strength in your season of doubt and unbelief. You will hope again where you once lost hope.

This book was given to Asia through her own personal sufferings to aid you with yours. "I Still Believe," is for those in the Faith, outside the Faith and for those who need to get back in the Faith. "I Still Believe," " is God's way of speaking to you right where you are and reminding you that He is not finished with you yet, regardless of where you are now or where you have been. It is your time now to Still Believe.

YaQuis B, Shelley
Sr. Pastor of The Hand of the Lord International Church
Founder of Branch Outreach Center
Author of "I Am Tamar"

#Preface

2017, is the year of Victory!! God's timing is perfect in releasing this book. My prayer is that this book takes your faith to another level and that you develop a STILL believe on the inside of you that no matter what you face you will still trust God. I pray that this book also stirs up faith in the faithless. Maybe you don't believe, maybe you have lost your faith, maybe life has hit you in such a way you have lost all hope. Somehow, God has placed this book in your hands. May it encourage you and impart life and faith into your heart .May it enable you to understand the Sovereignty of God that you may trust Him even when you don't understand Him. God has always been and will always be greater than the opposition we face. We can rest assured that despite what it looks like, in Him we have the Victory!

#IStillBelieve

I remember waking up to a lot of missed calls and text messages, only to call my younger sister back not prepared for the news I was about to receive. My older sister, who was pregnant at the time, had been rushed to the hospital. Her blood pressure caused her to have stroke and she was in a coma. My family was faced with the question of saving her or the baby. Thankfully, the doctors were able to get enough pressure off of my sister's brain to stabilize her and deliver my youngest niece, Destin.

I jumped up putting on my clothes as fast as I could and rushed to the hospital. I prayed that everything was going to be okay and that this would just be a "wake-up call". I hoped that this occurred just to bring our family closer together. When I arrived, the doctor came into my sister's room showing the family x-rays of internal bleeding. The stroke caused a blood vessel to burst and the internal bleeding covered a large portion of her brain. There were low chances of her recovering, but if there was a chance I was standing on that. I called my entire family on a fast and I sat in the hospital for three days, eating nothing, refusing to leave my sister's room. I couldn't even bring myself to leave the room to see my niece, the new life God had given us. I was determined to believe God for my sister's healing. I played one song on repeat called Healer by Hillsong.

"I believe You're my healer
I believe You are all I need
I believe You're my portion
I believe You're more than enough for me
Jesus, You're all I need
Nothing is impossible for You
Nothing is impossible
Nothing is impossible for You
You hold my world in Your hands,"

What I realize now, is this song was more for me than it was for her. I reminded God of how faithful I had been in serving Him. I wasn't out here in sin. I had given my life to Him, striving to obey and stay in His will. And at this moment, I needed Him now more than ever. In some way, I felt like God owed me and I was placing a demand upon Him. I needed Him to heal my sister.

I didn't care what the doctors were saying. I knew He was God and nothing was impossible for Him. I prayed, fasted and spoke the word of God over her life. I wanted to see a miracle. I wanted to experience the miracles I read about. I needed God to move on my behalf.

During this time, I had someone tell me that God didn't do miracles like that anymore. Maybe they had accepted the loss and they didn't want to hope and be disappointed. But not me, the statement made me angry and so I prayed harder, "God prove them wrong. You got to prove them wrong". As the psalmist said, "Prove the doubters wrong, you're still mighty and strong" ---Deon Kipping.

After 3 days in the hospital and no signs of recovery we were forced to make a decision. It was Resurrection Sunday 2014 and I thought for sure, if God was going to move this would be the day. We made the decision to pull the plug April 20th, 2014. I still believed even after the plug was pulled. I believed God until my sister's last breath and they were rolling her lifeless body out of the hospital room. I must have been in shock, because I still couldn't come to grips that my sister was really gone.

I felt foolish. Not only for myself, but I told other people to believe. I questioned

God, "Why didn't you make believers out of those who doubted you, instead of allowing doubt to enter those who believed you? You are God. Was this too hard for you?" I was angry and disappointed. I literally felt like God failed me.

Then I had questions of, "Why? I mean Why?" This story doesn't have a happy ending. My sister has five kids, who are now motherless. So many things were left undone and left unsaid. There were conversations that needed to happen. Forgiveness and healing that needed to take place within my family. Why now God? The timing felt very off.

Then there came the regret. I began thinking back to the last conversation we had, and if only I would have known that it would have been our last, what I would have said. I wouldn't have allowed our differences to wedge a gap between us. I would have spent more time with her. I then found myself looking for someone to blame. I began lashing out at my mother. What if she would have made different decisions? My emotions were all over the place. I was grieving the loss of today, while still trying to have some hope for tomorrow.

God is faithful and He is close to the broken hearted. I remember being in my room one day depressed and confused. God began to minister to me. At what point did He stop being God because He didn't do what I wanted Him to? Is God not Sovereign? And when did I become owner of "my sister."

You know, we put "my" at the front of things to signify ownership. I was angry as if my sister belonged to me. The fact is my sister did not belong to me. She always belonged to God. We all belong to God and at some point, we all will return to God. Our job is to be good stewards of the time and the people He has entrusted us with while we are here.

We love our loved ones, in our own selfishness, we never what to see them leave us. We don't want to experience life without them, but one day we will. One day someone is going to experience life without you. Death is a part of life. We weren't created to live here forever. One day we must return to God and give account of how we lived out our lives here on earth. The tricky part about it is we don't know when. We don't know how.

Most of the time we struggle with the "when" and the "how", but we don't get to choose our birth and we don't get to choose our death. What we do have control over is the dash in between birth-death. I was hit with another question.

Will I still trust God even when I don't understand Him?

This was a pivotal time in my life. I could have chosen to turn away from God or to turn to Him. The foundation of any relationship is trust and communication. I was at a point where I didn't want to pray and I doubted God because I felt that He let me down.

God reminded me of His faithfulness, even to Job in the Bible. A man that was considered righteous and lost everything, but was later restored. For every scripture that encourages us to believe there is another one that encourages us to **Still Believe**. Not only is God a physical healer, He's also an internal and emotional healer.

He is a healer of grief. In fact, He bore and overcame grief because He knew we are going to experience loss in this life.

God gave me the scripture, "For we walk by faith and not by sight" (2Corinthians 5:7) and birthed #IStillBelieve in me. To "Still" believe points to the fact that something has occurred or happened to challenge or destroy your belief. Belief is connected to hope. You believe what you hope for. When what you hope for is no longer there, your faith is challenged. The Bible says, "*Hope deferred makes the heart sick.*" (Proverbs 13:12) But God! God has a purpose. God has a plan.

What the enemy desires to use to destroy you, God will use to deliver you. The opposition that desires to weaken you, God will use to strengthen you. God will take your misery and birth your ministry. He will turn your pain into power. God can and will turn "it" around and use it for your good and for His Glory. Whatever "it" is for you. Maybe it's not the death of a loved one, maybe it's a broken marriage, a broken relationship, a lost job or career. Maybe someone hurt you or abused you. Whatever "it" is there is still hope for you. There is still hope for your family. There is still hope for your future. There is still hope for your life!

God has given me a message of Faith, the kind that must be unwavering. What we believe, who we believe, and why we believe determines the life we live. It distinguishes between the victim and the victor; the hopeful and the hopeless. Here is what faith in God does:

Faith destroys faulty belief systems.

Faith demolishes strongholds.

Faith makes you whole.

Faith unlocks miracles.

Faith moves mountains.

Great Faith produces Great Works.

Where there is Faith, there is deliverance.

Where there is Faith, there is Healing.

Faith produces transformation.

Faith gives strength to endure.

Faith gives power to overcome.

Faith is the Gateway to Victory.

Our faith is under attack because of what its connected to it. May the chapters ahead encourage, strengthen and fortify faith in your heart and life, that no matter what you face you will **Still Believe**.

#FaithOverGrief

"Come to me, all you who are weary and burden, and I will give you rest."- Matthew 11:28

"He sent forth His word to heal them and deliverer them from their destruction."- Psalm 107:20

Grief is described as deep sorrow; suffering, mental suffering, painful regrets or distress over affliction or loss. Although always associated with death, grief comes in many ways. If simplified it can be described as a broken heart, often the type that can shake your whole world and literally knock the breath out of you. Grief causes a person to be weary and sorrowful, developing a weight and hindrance in moving forward. Heavy hearts become burdens and if not properly dealt with lead to bitterness, despair and hopelessness; stuck in the past with no hope for the future.

While some people experience grief, others never stop grieving. They allow their whole lives to pass them by never allowing themselves to be healed. They allow their pain to become their identity. Existing but never living. But thanks be to God, who gives a solution to those who are weary and burden. God promises to give rest, comfort and peace in exchange of our burdens. (Matthew 11:28) God sent forth His word and Jesus (the word made flesh) to heal, restore and give us hope even in the midst of our grief.

We live in a grieving world. Everywhere we look there is pain and affliction. Hurting people who are hurting people. It's important to understand the cause and the solution to our grief. There is grief that we all will experience because of the sin. (the fall of Adam and Eve) This grief includes death and the fruit of our sinful nature. There is also grief that comes with following Jesus. The path of trusting Jesus is not trouble and problem free. In fact, Jesus said we will experience suffering, but there is a promise connected to our pain.

Original Sin

The term "original sin" originates from the fall of Adam and Eve. The moment Adam and Eve disobeyed God in the garden everything shifted. It brought about sin and death. Where the world knew no sin, no pain, no suffering, no grief and no death because of sin we will all experience it. It's important to understand sin brings grief. It brings grief to us and to others.

The decisions of Adam and Eve show us that our decisions don't just affect us but everyone connected to us, whether we choose to make good decisions or poor ones. Someone will reap the benefits or lack thereof. What's wonderful about it is, although the decisions of another person has the ability to affect us, their decisions do not have the power to hold us, to stop us, or prevent us from fulfilling our purpose and reaching our destiny. It's the decision of God, in sending His son to die for us, that liberates us and gives us hope.

"For just as through the disobedience of the one man the many were made sinners, so also through the obedience of the one man the many will be made righteous."- (Romans 5:19)

Death

Sin brought death but faith brings eternal life. Many people don't want to talk about death. They are fearful of dying. I heard someone say, "Everybody wants to go to heaven but nobody wants to die to get there." This is so true! Not only do we not want to die, we don't want to think about anyone close to us dying. We live our lives trying to protect the ones we love. The truth is, death is a part of life. Because of sin the world is no longer the perfect place God intended. For those who have accepted Christ, we accept the reality that earth is not our home. We accept the reality that we are only here for a limited amount of time. Life on earth is temporary. Life is short and in the limited amount of time we have here we have a purpose to fulfill.

Although these things are true, it doesn't fix or change the fact that death brings grief. It hurts. Nobody wants to lose a loved one. It alters your entire life and feels like a part of you is missing. It can shake the very core of your being. Pain has a way of taking you to a deep, dark and hopeless place, but when we apply faith to our pain we allow the healer to come in.

Some people hold on to grief thinking that if they stop grieving, they stop loving or caring about the person they lost. This is not the case. Acceptance doesn't mean you have forgotten about them, you just have chosen to live even when it feels you can't live without them. Christ allows us to get through what we can't seem to get over. In

Him we have hope. We have peace.

Naomi experienced grief when her husband and two sons died. The bible says she blamed God and became bitter.

"And she said unto them, Call me not Naomi, call me Mara: for the Almighty hath dealt very bitterly with me." (Ruth 1:20)

There is a temptation to blame God and become bitter when things don't go as we want or expect them to go. Many people get angry with God and some choose to deny His existence altogether. They turn away from Him, reject the truth and turn to sin. Sin, the very thing that causes death and grief. (Genesis 2:17-18)

A pastor once said, "Just because God is blamed doesn't mean He is guilty." God grieves too! (Genesis 6:6) He has feelings too, He hurts just like we do, but I imagine on a far greater scale. That can be hard to grasp when we look at God as being all powerful and a God who has everything within His control. Why would He allow things to happen that would not only inflict pain upon us but also upon Himself?

I believe that although God is a God in control, He's not a controlling God and that everyone has the power to choose. (Joshua 24:15) Sometimes our own choices lead to pain. I also understand He is an eternal God with an eternal perspective. Why certain things happen, why certain people suffer, I may never know. We may never know. But while we are consumed with life here on earth, He's preparing us for a place that is far greater in heaven. A place where there is no pain, no suffering, no death.

Most people believe death is the worst thing that could happen to a person but the truth is the worst thing that could happen is not death but eternal separation from God. The worst thing that could happen is dying without giving your life to Christ. The worst thing that could happen is not experiencing a temporary death but an eternal one. God in His foreknowledge knew that Adam and Eve would sin and that death would come so He put something in place, Eternal life. Faith tells us that we will see them again!

Naomi became so bitter she changed her name. Her name meaning "Joy/pleasantness" but she changed her named to "Mara" meaning bitterness. Grief is not the problem, it's how we deal with our grief. Naomi chose bitterness. She felt forsaken and rejected by God. Even in her anger and bitterness, God had a plan.

God connected her with Ruth, her widowed daughter- in law and a loyal friend who did not leave her side. Her connection to Ruth showed forth Gods favor in her life. Ruth married Boaz some kin to Naomi and her family was restored. (Ruth 4:1-22) While we only see what's in front of us now, God sees the entire picture. When we see pain, He sees restoration!

Sinful Nature

"Behold, I was shapen in iniquity; and in sin did my mother conceive me." - Psalm 51:5

Everyone is born into sin and shaped into iniquity; we entered this world with a sinful nature. We are dead in our sins, prone to do sinful destructive things until we accept Christ.

"As for you, you were dead in your transgressions and sins, in which you used to live when you followed the ways of this world and of the ruler of the kingdom of the air, the spirit who is now at work in those who are disobedient." Ephesians 1:1-2

"When you were dead in your sins and in the uncircumcision of your flesh, God made you alive with Christ." Colossians 2:13

Sin- inflicted suffering is selfish and deceptive, with the person not realizing that the present pleasure or temporary relief will only lead to corruption, destruction and ultimately death. Disobedience causes suffering. God tells us not to do certain things not as a means of control but because He knows the outcome. He knows that the result will lead to pain, not only to us but to others.

Sexual Abuse

Tamar was King David's daughter and she experienced sin inflicted grief when she was tricked and raped at the hand of her half-brother Absalom. Absalom allowed lust and perversion to overtake him. After raping Tamar, he rejected her. When she finally told what happened she was told to keep quiet. The bible says she tore her robe, which signified her identity. She became desolate, never to be heard of again. It was the custom for the king's daughter to wear robes which pointed to their royalty and purity. Tamar's abuse affected her entire life. (2 Sam 13:1-22)

Just like Tamar I experienced sexual abuse. This offense and grief lead me down a path of self-hatred, rejection, misplaced identity and homosexuality. The abuse to me confirmed the childhood insecurities and lies I believed about myself. I developed a disdain for myself and for men. The grief of experiencing loss, a loss of my innocence and identity allowed me to pick up male characteristics.

I created the person I wanted to be because I didn't like who I was. I gave myself my own identity and changed my name. I introduced myself as "Fresh" a rap name that I was known by in the homosexual community. Because I didn't know how to deal with my grief, it led me to an identity and lifestyle totally outside of the will of God. Where has your grief led you?

Sexual abuse is such a grievous offense that comes with so many different emotions. It affects a person physically, mentally, emotionally and spiritually. It attacks the very core of one's identity, often turning them into a person they were never created to be. Grief never comes alone; it usually brings its friends bitterness, guilt and shame.

Most people who experience sexual abuse usually have this one thing in common: they blame themselves. They reject themselves and see no value in themselves. Thinking, "if I was valued this wouldn't have happened to me or somebody would have protected me." If you were raped or sexually abused I want you to know it was not your fault! Nothing gives a person the right to violate you.

There is no justification for sexual abuse. In fact, God forbids it. (Deuteronomy 22)

For those of us who have been abused to walk in liberty, forgiveness is the remedy. This often includes forgiving those who were supposed to protect you, forgiving those who violated you, forgiving those who failed to defend you and forgiving yourself for decisions you think you should or shouldn't have made.

You can overcome the effects of sexual abuse and be all that God has called you to be. If you need someone to help aid you in the process located in the back of this book is a resource you can reach out to.

Faith Inflicted Grief - Jesus

Though there are many examples of people in the bible who were considered righteous and experienced grief, Jesus is the ultimate example.

His grief led to our victory. Jesus is the reason we can put faith over grief.

"He is despised and rejected of men; a man of sorrows, and acquainted with grief: and we hid as it were our faces from him; he was despised, and we esteemed him not. Surely, he hath borne our griefs, and carried our sorrows: yet we did esteem him stricken, smitten of God, and afflicted. But he was wounded for our transgressions; he was bruised for our iniquities: the chastisement of our peace was upon him; and with his stripes we are healed."- (Isaiah 53)

Because of what Jesus did through his death, burial and resurrection, as a believer, grief does not have dominion over us.

"We don't grieve like the world as if we have no hope."- (1 Thessalonians 4:13)

Faith-inflicted suffering is the suffering that comes with obedience and doing what is right and just. With this grief we experience hope and joy. It doesn't mean it feels good or we enjoy what we are facing but we understand that as believers we have an expected outcome. There is a promise past the pain.

Anybody that accomplished anything great in God experienced suffering, grief and disappointment along the way. Their hope was not in the journey or the process (though it was necessary) but in the destination and outcome. Jesus suffered and died so that we may be saved, healed and delivered. Faith-inflicted suffering is always worth it. It always repays more than what is lost. It's always beneficial. We can hold on to the promise because we know and trust the promise keeper.

"For I reckon that the sufferings of this present time are not worthy to be compared with the glory that will be revealed in us"- Romans 8:18

"I have told you these things, so that in me you may have peace. In this world you will have trouble. But take heart! I have overcome the world."- John 16:33

#FaithOverFlesh

"Beloved, I urge you as sojourners and exiles to abstain from passions of the flesh, which wage war against your soul." - 1 Peter 2:11

"This I say then, walk in the Spirit, and ye shall not fulfill the lust of the flesh." - Galatians 5:16

I believe the biggest fight we have is not against the devil or others. It's the war against self; a fight not from without, but from within. The war and battle against our own flesh and sinful nature, between what we want to do and what we know is right. The part of us that seeks temporary pleasure over eternal satisfaction. The part of us that can't be redeemed or saved, but must be brought to death every day of our lives.

The flesh, our sinful nature, must constantly be

brought under submission to the word of God. The conviction must outweigh the pleasure. The desire to please God must outweigh the desire to please self. We must purse purity and holiness, making no provision for the flesh. Lest we lay dormant, bound by sin, sexual immorality, vile affections, lust and perversion. Now unto Christ who is able, to enable us to crucify the works of the flesh where there dwells no good thing.

Temptation

We are a three part being - **body, soul** and **spirit**. Our flesh, also known as our **body,** is the part of us that makes us legal on earth. This is the seat of our temptation and sinful nature.

Our **soul** is made up of our mind, will and emotions. Jesus died for our souls, and temptation often comes in the form of our flesh to lead our souls astray.

Our **spirit** allows us to commune with God and know Him personally. Where our souls were created to be ruled by our spirits, everything got out of order due to sin. Now, there is a consistent conflict between our flesh and the spirit. Our flesh says one thing, but our spirit says another and both desire to rule our souls.

There is a war against our souls, for our soul. Paul describes it best

"The sinful nature wants to do evil, which is just the opposite of what the Spirit wants. And the Spirit gives us desires that are the opposite of what the sinful nature desires. These two forces are constantly fighting each other...."- Galatians 5:17-19

Temptation comes in many forms which are the lust of the flesh, the lust of the eyes and the pride of life (1 John 2:16). Here are some brief descriptions and examples.

Lust of the flesh- physical pleasure from sinful activity.
Ex. sexual sins, gossip, physical violence, drug use (Galatians 5:19-21)

Lust of the eyes- to look upon things we shouldn't. To desire things based on visual appeal.
Ex. Coveting, pornography, status and material possession

Pride of Life- arrogance, pride in what you possess.
Ex. Desire for recognition, applause and status, boasting in achievements, gifts and possessions.

The bible also points to the fact that we are tempted when we are drawn away by our own lust. (James 1:14) So everybody is not tempted by the same things. What tempts you may not tempt the next person. But with every temptation God gives us an escape.

No temptation has overtaken you except what is common to mankind. And God is faithful; he will not let you be tempted beyond what you can bear. But when you are tempted, he will also provide a way out so that you can endure it. – (1 Corinthians 10:13)

God gives us a way to escape but we still hold the power to choose. Character, discipline, submission and obedience are only shown forth in the face of temptation. Temptation shows us where we really are and it exposes who we really are

.

Jesus gives us the perfect example of resisting temptation. The Bible says He was led in the wilderness and tempted of Satan. Because He died to His will and submitted to the will and word of the Father, He resisted the devil. When we are led by our flesh and sinful desires, we give away the power to overcome the devil and ignore the way of escape. We actually come in agreement with Satan to defy God's will.

Satan will always wrap his will in our self-will. He uses our flesh and sinful nature against us. Because he is a trickster, it will look appealing but always lead to destruction. Character, submission and obedience are only shown forth in the face of temptation. We can't get rid of our flesh but we can learn to discipline it.

The lack of discipline will lead to disobedience. Most people go to God due to how their disobedience has affected them, instead of approaching Him broken, because of how their disobedience has affected God. When we don't obey God, or put Him in His rightful place, we can always expect hurt, pain and disappointment. You must repent from how you got yourself into the things and situations that you now need deliverance from. As long as you're the victim of your disobedience, you will never be the victor of it.

The Mind

Let's not be mistaken, although we war against the flesh, the weapons of our warfare are not carnal, but mighty through Christ Jesus in the pulling down of strongholds. (2 Corinthians 10:4).

Where are these strongholds formulated? In our minds. Your body can do nothing without your mind. Your mind tells your body what to do. That's why when we give our lives to Christ, we must change the way we think. There must be a change of mind. Our mindset needs to change because the things we use to do with our bodies, we can't do any more.

"The mind governed by the flesh is hostile to God; it does not submit to God's law, nor can it do so." -
(Romans 8:7)

The bible says, *do not conform to this world but be*

ye transformed by the renewing of your mind. (Romans 12:2) What does that mean? Don't do what the world does, they are led by their flesh. As for you, allow yourself to be changed (actions and behaviors) by renewing your mind by His word. If our mind is what control our bodies we must be mindful of what we feed our minds.

Feelings

"The heart is deceitful above all things and beyond cure. Who can understand it?"- Jeremiah 17:9

The world tells us, "Follow your heart", "Do what you feel". The problem with that is, our emotions are unstable and our feelings lie. Have you ever felt very strongly about something? As in, no one could tell you any different. You were completely fixed on how you felt about it, only to find out what you felt or believed was not the truth after all. That can be devastating and even dangerous when we trust what we feel over the word of God. Feelings can override our conscience and ignore the signs that God gives us to let us know we are on the wrong track. Feelings will put you in situations that only faith can get you out of.

Feelings are defined as the state of emotion and reaction. Wow, this points to the fact that our feelings don't just originate on their own but are a reaction to something. Our feelings are often a response to what we see and what we think, they can be carnal and unpredictable. These feelings must be brought under subjection to the will of God. Our minds must be renewed so that our emotions don't rule us.

Faith is not your feelings. In fact, God will allow your feelings to be hurt to fix your heart. I was in a relationship where I had idolized the person I was with. Not knowing it, I had made this person my god. I had gone through failed relationship after relationship, I realized I put everyone and everything first but Him. God allowed this person to fail me so that I could see Him. God is infallible and loves us with such an everlasting love. He does everything with our best interest in mind. Nobody can and will ever be able to love us to the capacity of Christ.

Think about it....

When you're in a crisis, when you're scared for your life or when you need something only God can do, you don't call out for those things, relationships and people you put before God. You call out for God Himself, because you realize you need Him more than anything and anyone. Nobody can help you but Him. Nobody can fix it but Him. So why in the world would we put anything or anyone before Him? They can't save you. They will hurt you. They will not always be there for you, no matter how much they say they love you. They are human. They are limited. They are fallible. God is the only one who can make good on the promise of never leaving us or forsaking us.

Sex, Fornication and Masturbation

I know it's touchy, but #IStillBelieve: We have the Victory. Lol. When we talk about flesh, this seems to be one of the biggest struggles among believers. Staying pure and holy - oh the struggle, to disciple our bodies and bring our flesh under subjection. When I got saved, I was use to having sex. I was use to being in the bed with someone else. Because I was not married or in the will of God, fornication was a part of my sinful lifestyle. My flesh had been introduced to something that it enjoyed and just because I had received Christ and changed my thinking toward sex, didn't mean my body was going to stop crying out for something it was use to having. Jesus makes this plain, He said...

"If you desire to be a follower of me deny yourself, take up your cross and follow me."- Matthew 16:24

Because denying myself is a part of me being a follower of Christ, I can't entertain things in my mind that will cause my flesh to sin. We have to know our triggers. We can't put ourselves in compromising situations thinking that we are "Strong". Compromising situations lead to compromise and pride goes before destruction and a haughty spirit before a fall. (Proverbs 16:18) We must put no confidence in our flesh.

If you think you stand, take heed least you fall. -1 Corinthians 10:12

Sex

Sex was God's design. He created sex. He made it for procreation and also made it enjoyable. Sex was created to be between a husband and wife.

"For this reason, a man will leave his father and mother and be united to his wife, and the two will

become one flesh.' So they are no longer two, but one flesh."- Matthew 10:7-8

Sex of itself, is not sinful. It's the context in which it is used. We live in a generation where we have perverted sex through fornication, homosexuality and bestiality. Pornography is at all-time high, a billion-dollar industry. We have sex toys and unnatural ways to find pleasure. Sex motivated by lust and self-gratification has led many people to ruins. It has broken up many marriages and opened the doors for many addictions. You're not living a life of freedom when you're continually controlled and driven by lust.

With a society that is so sexually explicit, parents and guardians, need to talk to their children about sex. You'll find that most of the time, they know more than you think. Nowadays kids are introduced and exposed to so much, from the media and school to neighborhood friends. They need to know the truth about sex and why it's important to stay sexually pure.

Fornication

This happens when we step outside of the boundaries God created for sex. Fornication is when you have sex with someone who is not your spouse. A lot of times we see the word of God as a means to control us, not understanding it's to protect us. Often times the protection is from demonic spirits of lust, perversion, unwed pregnancies, heartbreak and different physical illnesses you can subject yourself to by being out of the will of God. Nowadays there is HIV and so many STD's, some that doctors can't even find a cure for.

Fornication also creates ungodly soul ties. People find themselves tied to relationships that they need to break free from, but can't because their souls, (mind, will and emotions) have been entangled. They have become one with someone illegally. (Mark 10:8) When your mind and emotions are tied, you're unable to make wise decisions and choices. This explains how a person can stay in abusive relationship knowing they need to leave or stay with someone they know doesn't have their best interest. Soul-ties need to be broken so that individuals can break free.

A lot of people fornicate and call it love. Love would never cause you to sin against the God who created you. Therefore, you cannot "make love" with someone you are not married to. You are making lust. You're making sin.

"Then when lust hath conceived, it bringeth forth sin: and sin, when it is finished, bringeth forth death." James 1:15

When we step outside of the will of God, we open up ourselves to so much heartache and pain. We also miss out on what could be fruitful, successful and good relationships because we allow them to become lustful. Lust taints and corrupts relationships. Our Faith has to be in His will and not in what we feel.

Masturbation

I've heard many people try to argue about masturbation. Anyway, the subject is flipped, masturbation is impure and not God's design for sex. It's lustful and sinful. You're having sex with yourself. It's idolatry and self-pleasure. Most of the time masturbation is coupled with pornography and sex toys. This sin has led many people to become inventors of evil things. (Romans 1:30)

Society has perverted sex and has even exalted masturbation as to being normal, healthy and the safest form of sex. Masturbation opens all types of doors for demons to reside, a lot of times people become addicted to pornography and driven by the images they have seen. Pornography has broken marriages. Their partners have fallen into an illusion, and placed unrealistic expectations upon their spouse, finding they can never be pleased by them.

"I Beseech you therefore, brethren, by the mercies of God, that ye present your bodies a living sacrifice, holy, acceptable unto God, which is your reasonable service." Romans 12:1

A person can sin and at one-point feel conviction. Over time after not repenting but repeatedly participating in it, they no longer have a conviction about it. It doesn't mean it's no longer wrong. God will turn you over to a reprobate mind and you will begin to bear the fruit of your sin.

"And even as they did not like to retain God in their knowledge, God gave them over to a reprobate mind, to do those things which are not convenient "- Romans 1:28

Our flesh will never have our best interest. It will set us up for failure every time. It's not wise; it lives in the moment with no thought of the future. It's selfish, with no lasting benefits to self. The flesh, when given into, silences the voice of God and separates us from His presence. The flesh will have you make permanent decisions in temporary situations. It will bring about compromise and will cause you to forfeit the promises of God.

"Flee from sexual immorality. All other sins a person commits are outside the body, but whoever sins sexually, sins against their own body."- 1 Corinthians 6:18

Faith and Obedience go hand in hand. In fact, the bible says Faith without works is dead. (James 2:26) When it comes to our flesh, we have to go back to the basics of Christianity. Remind ourselves of scriptures that say, "If anyone wants to become my follower, he must deny himself, take up his cross, and follow me",(Matthew 16:24) or "Unless I wash you, you have no part with me". (John 13:8) We can't get away from denying ourselves, taking up our cross and allowing ourselves to be washed. I'm talking about DAILY. We don't ever get away from that. Denying ourselves is a qualification of being a follower of Christ. Faith must be over our flesh and through the help of the Holy Spirit we have the power to live Spirit led lives.

#FaithOverRejection

For I know the plans I have for you," declares the LORD, "plans to prosper you and not to harm you, plans to give you hope and a future. - Jeremiah 29:11

You intended to harm me, but God intended it for good to accomplish what is now being done, the saving of many lives. - Genesis 50:20

This hits close to home and I finally realize how detrimental the spirit of rejection has been in my life. Rejection comes in so many different forms, from the rejection of others, self- rejection and the fear of rejection. All of these taint how you view yourself and torment your mind. Rejection will have you being someone God never called you to be, doing things God never called you to do and being places God never called you to be. After much studying, reading and examining my own life, I'm convinced that you must put faith over rejection.

It's through our faith in God we come to know who we are and know how accepted and beloved we are. It's through faith we overcome the spirit of rejection.

Rejection

Rejection is described as the refusal to accept and the dismissing of. If simply described, rejection is the absence of acceptance. We all want to be accepted but the truth of the matter is we all will experience rejection. When rejection is taken personally and internalized, it can enter our hearts and minds becoming a foundational issue that hinders us from being who God called us to be. Some of the most common ways (not all) that rejection enters our lives are

1. Being denied by a parent while in the womb
2. Abandoned or put up for adoption
3. Neglect or the absence of a parent

4. Abuse. (sexual, mental, physical, emotional)

The spirit of rejection can also enter our lives through the lack of affirmation and the absence of someone speaking into our life who God has called us to be. Children need affirmation. This is supposed to be the primary job of the father. Fathers are to hear from God concerning their child and to name and affirm the child according to their purpose. Because of the absence of Godly parent's children grow up not knowing who they are. If they don't learn at home who they were created to be, the world will tell them who they should be.
Rejection is better handled when you know who you are.

We all will experience rejection in some way shape or form, but there is a huge difference from experiencing rejection and internalizing rejection. This is where everything you do, strive for and become is from a place of rejection. You're motivated by rejection. These people tend to find their value in people and things. They subconsciously believe if they don't possess certain things, they don't have value. They spend all their money on things and appearances to make them feel good about themselves or to appear to others as being important. They try to apply an external solution to an inward brokenness.

Our value is not in what we have; it's who we are that makes us valuable. I wasted so much money buying things and clothes trying to compensate for my lack of identity. But I'm encouraged today to know that life does not exist in the abundance of things that we possess. (Luke 12:15)

Self-Rejection

Often time rejection leads to self-rejection. I think this is the worst form of rejection, when a person begins to turn on themselves and believes the lies and thoughts of the enemy. They come in agreement with those who have treated them less than. Bullies are known for this; antagonizing and tearing people down. This is the work of Satan. When we reject ourselves, we believe the opinions of others instead of the opinion of the one who made us and created us with purpose, God.

Self-rejection can enter through shame. It happens when you do something you're ashamed of and you don't forgive yourself. You began to reject yourself and hate yourself for your actions and choices. If God can extend grace, mercy and forgiveness to us, we must be able to receive it and forgive ourselves.

Self-rejection can come when someone shames you or does something that brings shame to your life. They make choices that embarrass or humiliate you. Abuse is a common way Satan produces shame and self–rejection through physical abuse, mental abuse, emotional abuse and sexual abuse. The bible tells the story of Tamar, the daughter of David, and how she was sexually abused by her brother, Absalom. After he abused her, he rejected her.

Howbeit he would not hearken unto her voice: but, being stronger than she, forced her, and lay with her. Then Amnon hated her exceedingly; so that the hatred wherewith he hated her was greater than the love wherewith he had loved her. And Amnon said unto her, Arise, be gone. 16 And she said unto him, There is no cause: this evil in sending me away is greater than the other that thou didst unto me. But he would not hearken unto her. 17 Then he called his servant that ministered unto him, and said, Put now this woman out from me, and bolt the door after her. And Tamar put ashes on her head, and rent her garment of divers colours that was on her, and laid her hand on her head, and went on crying"- 2Samuel 13:15-17

I read this story many times before and it always stood out to me that she tore her robe, which signified a stripping of her identity. But before she tore her robe the bible says she poured ashes on her head. I never really dug into the ashes but this is important! The ashes symbolize the shame, the humiliation and self- abhorrence. Tamar became disgusted with herself and this caused her to strip her robe and identity. The abuse, the shame, the rejection led to her rejecting herself.

Self- Rejection opens the door to self-hatred and often leads to identity crisis. Its seen in those who live opposite from who they were meant to be. This is seen heavily in the LGBT community. When we see a person, who was born a male or female by God's design decide they no longer like the sex they are and desire to change it, they have rejected themselves. They don't like who they were created to be, so they take on the mannerisms, language and behaviors of the opposite sex. Some even go so far to go through with the procedure to become like the opposite sex. They change their names and how they identify themselves. This is self-rejection, but it's also rejection to the God who created them. It says to God you were wrong, you made a mistake. You put me in the wrong body.

"Woe unto him that striveth with his Maker! Let the potsherd strive with the potsherds of the earth. Shall the clay say to him that fashioneth it, What makest thou? or thy work, He hath no hands?"- Isaiah 45:9

I lived majority of my life dealing with this. I dressed and looked just like a boy. I carried so much shame and self- rejection from being sexually abused and bullied growing up. I didn't feel beautiful or feminine so I embraced a more masculine appearance, living a homosexual lifestyle. This led to a lot of attention, attention I never received dressing like a girl. I was rejecting who God created me to be and embracing a person I created. My own brokenness led to a lifestyle I was never meant to live.

Self–rejection can manifest in low self-esteem, depression, suicide, feelings of worthlessness and defeat. Self-rejection can be found in those who continually do things that hurt themselves. For example, those who cut themselves, have eating disorders, addictions or use drugs and alcohol. It can also be seen in those who stay in abusive situations and relationships. Self-rejection leads to self-sabotage.

Fear of Rejection

The fear of rejection will show up in one or two ways: self-pity and people pleasing or rebellion and isolation. John Eckhart in his book "Destroying the spirit of Rejection" gives great examples of this with two people from the bible, Ahab and Jezebel. Both give the inward and outward manifestations of rejection. Ahab resulted in self-pity and insecurity whereas, Jezebel was controlling, self-willed and stubborn both feared rejection (1Kings 21:4-7).

When people fear rejection, they do things that would prevent them from experiencing it. Some become people pleasers. They conform to the wishes of those around them, even when they don't want to. They do things that are outside of their character to fit in and be accepted.

I remember my niece coming home one day talking different. It wasn't a rude different, it was a "this is not you" different. We began to investigate. Who talks like this? Who have you been around that has caused you to act like them instead of being yourself? She was struggling with the fear of rejection. If I act like them and do what they do maybe they will accept me. The fear of rejection will cause you to be a person you are not for the sake of being accepted.

The fear of rejection can also take another turn. I will reject you before you reject me. Deep down inside this person wants to be accepted but because of the fear of rejection, they reject others. They are very critical of others and have built walls preventing them from having healthy relationships. These types of people can be very prideful and arrogant but the root is they are fearful of being rejected.

Rejected for Protection

Rejection is not always a bad thing. In fact as I look over my life and certain rejections I have faced, I'm thankful. It didn't feel good while it was taking place, in fact it hurt. But being rejected by others has shown me just how accepted I am by God. God will allow rejection for our protection. Maybe if you would have gotten what you wanted, it may have ruined your life. Maybe it would have caused a setback to where God is taking you. Maybe it would have led to heartbreak and turmoil.

I'm glad that job didn't come through, or that person didn't like me like I liked them. If God allowed everything I wanted to happen, I wouldn't be where I am now. I would have settled for less than what God has for me. Maybe you've experienced rejection because you're selected by God. And maybe what God has for you is far greater than you can imagine for yourself.

Rejection Apart of the Plan

I am reminded of a man in the Bible by the name of Joseph. God had great plans to prosper him and make him a ruler over his kinsmen, but the path to get there was full of rejection. Joseph gives us a great example of what it was like to be rejected and how God used it to bless him and prosper him.

Joseph kept a right heart, trusted God and remained faithful. He was sold into slavery by his own brothers. He was later lied on and thrown into prison. Through it all God favored Joseph, and those who rejected him later needed him.

God knows how to make your enemies your footstool. God elevated Joseph and when a great famine came to the land those who rejected him now needed him. Joseph helped them, he wasn't revengeful. God developed character in him that he could trust him to bless his enemies.

Faith allows us to trust Gods plan. All rejection is not bad rejection. When we place faith over rejection, we understand better the plan and love God has for us. He has plans of good, to give us hope and an expected end. (Jeremiah 29:11) God will take what the enemy meant for bad and use it for His Glory.

#FaithOverFear

" For God has not given us a spirit of Fear but of power, love and sound judgment." - 2 Timothy 1:7

"The fear of the LORD is the beginning of knowledge: but fools despise wisdom and instruction." - Proverbs 1:7

Fear can be paralyzing and tormenting, but it can also be protective. Fear can be the enemy of faith or can exist because of your faith. I believe that there is a fear that keeps us from fulfilling the will of God because we are afraid to trust Him, but there is also fear that keeps us in the will of God because we understand life without Him. If we are going to fear, let it be the fear connected to our faith. The fear that gives us an awe and reverence of God, not the fear that keep us doubtful, complacent and bound by unbelief. Above all let's live faith driven lives.

The Spirit of Fear

The spirit of fear is the enemy of faith in God. It makes you afraid. It produces worry, anxiety, and torment. There is no power, no love and no sound judgment when the spirit of fear is present. Fear brings doubt and uncertainty. It opposes of the power that God has given us to face what seems impossible and go forth when the odds are against us. It causes us to not truly be perfected in love.

Fear is self-preserving, while love is selfless and esteems others higher than itself. The spirit of fear robs us of a sound mind and peace. It opens the door to think about all the worst-case scenarios and keeps us doubtful and stagnant in decision-making. Fear produces procrastination and complacency.

Anxiety / Fear

There are so many ways that fear can plague your life. Some people have phobias and wrestle with anxiety. Anxiety is the expectation of a future threat, whereas fear is a response to a real perceived immediate threat. The crazy thing is we can fear and have anxiety about something that may never happen. The emotions of fear and anxiety can block a person from being able to fully assess a situation to find a hopeful and good ending.

Fear of Rejection/Fear of Failure

The fears that I have faced is the fear of rejection and the fear of failure. A lot of my fears have been imbedded in how I have viewed myself. My lack of identity caused me to fear rejection because I was insecure. I would reject others before they rejected me. I developed an "I don't care" attitude, fueled by pride.

I became a very hard person, never being able to say I was hurt because that made me feel vulnerable and weak, and I feared being taken advantage of. A lot of my fear stemmed from being sexually abused. I feared failure. I still must identify and deal with that fear when it tries to arise. I must ask myself, what am I being motivated by? Is this faith or fear?

The fear of failure will cause you to be performance oriented, trying to find value in your accomplishments and what you are doing instead of God. It will also cause you to shut down when faced with opposition, starting things but never completing anything. It will cause you to place unrealistic expectations upon yourself, despise small beginnings, and not give yourself room to grow and develop.

God continually tells His people in the bible to fear not and affirms them with His promises and presence.

Isaiah 41:10 - *"Fear thou not; for I [am] with thee: be not dismayed; for I [am] thy God: I will strengthen thee; yea, I will help thee; yea, I will uphold thee with the right hand of my right."*

Psalms 27:1-2 - *"The Lord is my light and my salvation; whom shall I fear? The Lord is the strength of my life; of whom shall I be afraid? `When the wicked, even mine enemies and my foes, came upon me to eat up my flesh, they stumbled and fell."*

Deuteronomy 31:6 - *"Be strong and of a good courage, fear not, nor be afraid of them: for the Lord thy God, he it is that doth go with thee; he will not fail thee, nor forsake thee."*

Isaiah 43:1 - *"But now thus saith the Lord that created thee, O Jacob, and he that formed thee, O Israel, Fear not: for I have redeemed thee, I have called thee by thy name; thou art mine."*

Jesus also rebukes the disciples for being fearful, and described it as being faithless.

Matthew 8: 24-26 says, "*And, behold, there arose a great tempest in the sea, insomuch that the ship was covered with the waves: but he was asleep. And his disciples came to him, and awoke him, saying, Lord, save us: we perish. And he saith unto them, Why are ye fearful, O ye of little faith? Then he arose, and rebuked the winds and the sea; and there was a great calm."*

Doubt and Unbelief

There is no victory without opposition. When faced with things beyond our control, we must trust the one who is in control! Peter walking on water shows us what happens when we take our eyes off Jesus. He became distracted, fearful, and began to sink.

"*Then Peter got down out of the boat, walked on the water and came toward Jesus. But when he saw the wind, he was afraid and, beginning to sink, cried out, "Lord, save me!" Immediately Jesus reached out his hand and caught him. "You of little faith," he said, "why did you doubt?"*— Matthew 14:29-31

Jesus went straight to the root of Peter's fear, and it was doubt and unbelief. Truth is, when we find ourselves overwhelmed with fear and anxiety it points to fact that we don't trust God. Peter saw the storm and in that moment, he viewed the storm as being more powerful than Christ. What I like about Peter is, though his doubt caused him to sink, his faith pulled him up. He knew to call on the Lord to save him. Faith is the key to every unlocked miracle. When we believe the word of God over what we face, it gives us courage, hope and strength.

This is such a fearful time for this world and nation. But we can't allow the storms of this life to move us from faith into fear, but rather fear into faith. Fear into repentance and right standing with

God. We must ask ourselves, where have we placed our hope? Is it in the things we possess? Is it in our government? Is it in us? Is it in FEMA or Red Cross? Is it in DACA? Is it in others? Is it our abilities, or our wealth? Is it in our very own lives? All these things are temporary and when these things are gone, denied or delayed, people fear. They panic. When what they have placed their security in is not so secure, people begin to worry and fret. They have no peace and often make bad decisions in the state of desperation. We must place our hope in something greater, the One who is eternal, Jesus!

Believing, receiving, and understanding God's love, purpose, and plan for us eliminates the spirit of fear. In fact, the bible says, "Perfect Love casteth out all fear..." (1John 4:18). God is with us and He promises to never leave or forsake us. There is protection in our faith and obedience. It doesn't mean we are never going to face troubled times, but we understand that our life is in His hands. Our relationship with God prepares us, strengthens us, and equips us, that we may be confident in His promises.

I Respect Him

The Bible speaks of fear in a different context. It tells us to "fear the Lord". As we dig deeper into the definition we will find that fearing the Lord does not mean to be afraid of Him but to reverence, respect and stand in awe of Him. This fear in Hebrew is translated as *yirah*. When we *yirah* the Lord we obey and respect Him. We know and understand that He is not telling us anything wrong, and He has our best interest at heart. We reverence Him because we understand that His word is not there to control us, but to protect and perfect us. We are in awe of Him because we understand the consequence of our sin and through His love for us He died that we may be liberated from the bondage and consequence of it. We shouldn't be afraid of God, but afraid of sin.

If your parents were anything like my parents, growing up you had a *yirah* for them. My dad has a way of correcting me that brings me to a heart of repentance. I can count on one hand the times he has physically reprimanded me. He didn't have to whip me. His voice and the sound of his displeasure would bring me to tears. Not because I was afraid of Him but because I love him. It hurt me to disappoint him or let him down. I wanted to make him proud and I wanted him to be pleased with me. Because he was not a very vocal father growing up, I knew that if he was correcting me, I had really done something wrong.

All his corrections were for my benefit and most of them got me out of and saved me from a world of trouble. Him correcting me was far better than the world correcting me. The Bible says that God chastises those in whom He loves. God's chastisement is always to bring us to a heart of repentance. It's not for evil or malice. God is a loving Father and if we fear anything it should be the wages of our sin and disobedience. When we don't allow Him to correct us through our conscience, through conviction of the Holy Spirit or through others, we open ourselves up to reap the consequences of our decisions. With an unrepentant heart we reap destruction, death, pain, and if not corrected in time, hell.

Sometimes what we fear comes upon us because of our disobedience. (I think it should be made known that hell is real and that God sends no one to hell. Hell was created for satan and the fallen angels, but whom we choose to follow in time, is who will follow in eternity.)

Fearing the Lord is always connected with obedience and the benefits/consequences of not obeying Him.

Proverbs 1:7 - *"The fear of the LORD [is] the beginning of knowledge: [but] fools despise wisdom and instruction."*

Deuteronomy 10:12 - *"And now, Israel, what doth the LORD thy God require of thee, but to fear the LORD thy God, to walk in all his ways, and to love him, and to serve the LORD thy God with all thy heart and with all thy soul."*

Proverbs 14:27 - *"The fear of the LORD [is] a fountain of life, to depart from the snares of death."*

Proverbs 14:26 - *"In the fear of the LORD [is] strong confidence: and his children shall have a place of refuge."*

The *yirah* of God dispels any spirit of fear that would desire to prevent us from moving in faith. In fact, the reverence and awe of God is formed through our faith and trust in Him. The perfect love of God casts out all fear so that we may walk in faith over every storm and obstacle that would come to scare us out of the will of God.

#FaithOverFailure

"If we confess our sins, he is faithful and just to forgive us our sins and to cleanse us from all unrighteousness." - 1 John 1:9

"My flesh and my heart may fail, but God is the strength of my heart and my portion forever."- Psalms 73:26

Just because things didn't work the way you intended doesn't mean you're a failure. Just because you have made mistakes doesn't mean you're a failure. Just because people have abused, neglected and mistreated you doesn't mean you're a failure. Just because you have failed doesn't mean you're a failure. Failing shows us our need and dependence for God. There is no failure in Him. And when we are in God there is no failure in us. Mistakes become lessons learned and opportunities to grow, not a badge we wear to identify us.

Sometimes God allows failure to show us we are outside of His will, or that what we are pursuing is not His will for us. We can expect failure when we step outside of the will of God. Failure sometimes shows us that God must be the source. There is no success apart from God. He is the epitome of success, lasting success and eternal success.

In this chapter I want to tackle guilt, shame and defeat. I have watched these things rob so many people, including myself. When these things aren't properly addressed you remain a victim when God has called you to be a victor. You remain stuck in the past, allowing your mistakes to become your identity, repeating the past and unable to move forward. When we understand who we are, value and forgive ourselves, we can walk in the freedom that faith allows.

Guilt

According to the dictionary, guilt is when a person believes or realizes that he or she has compromised his or her own standards of conduct or has violated a universal moral standard and bears significant responsibility for that violation. Guilt is the recognition that you have done something wrong. We should feel guilty about our wrong doings, it's a problem when you can do things that are wrong and sinful and not feel bad about them. Where there is no conviction, there is no conversion. We must see that something is wrong in order to implement change.

Some people however have a seared conscience. They may have once felt guilty about something but after ignoring the conviction they no longer feel convicted or guilty. The Bible describes this as God giving them over to a reprobate mind. (Romans 12:2)

There are those who only feel guilty because they got caught. The Bible describes this as worldly sorrow. They don't truly feel bad about what they have done; they just regret the consequences of it. It's a selfish kind of sorrow. This sorrow doesn't produce a change of heart or lifestyle. Then there is a Godly sorrow and this sorrow leads to repentance, not only does the person see the effects of their decisions but they see the importance of turning away from what has led them astray. (2 Corinthians 7:10-10)

Before I knew my lifestyle wasn't the way God intended. My guilt did not lead me to repentance because although I knew I was wrong, I figured everybody else was wrong too. I projected my guilt upon others and justified my wrong decisions. I found a just cause for doing what I was doing. I've learned that when we can give an explanation or excuse for why, it eases our conscience to makes us feel less guilty about what we have done. There is no repentance until we remove the excuses and say, "I'm wrong, I repent, let me make choices that will fix it."

It's unhealthy and unproductive to know you've been guilty of something and continue to beat up on yourself. Repent, forgive yourself and stop punishing yourself for past mistakes. Forgiving yourself doesn't mean you disregard what you have done and those you have hurt. It means you acknowledge that you were guilty and you repent. You extend your apologies to those who were affected, even if they don't accept your apology. You choose to turn from those things you were doing, and make different and better choices. Waddling in your mistakes and continually punishing yourself benefits no one. Forgive yourself and live in peace knowing you're making steps to become a better person each day.

Guilt can also come with unrealistic expectations. I have had to learn that a lot of what I have faced has been unrealistic expectations that I placed on others and myself. To think you will never make a mistake, fail or go through a bad experience is unrealistic. To think that people will never disappoint you or let you down is unrealistic. But how we view it, recover and grow from it makes us who we are.

I've even been in situations where I would get mad and beat myself up because I felt that I wasn't growing fast enough, but how many times does a child fall down before it learns to walk? The child doesn't just quit and give up because they can't walk on the first try. Walking is something new to them. Walking by faith and living for Jesus is something new to us, when we first give our lives to God. We don't willingly sin, but you go through moments of immaturity. There are things we learn and grow from in stages of immaturity.

We cannot change our past, but we can repeat it if we don't learn to forgive ourselves and move forward. We can't live in our mistakes; we must have the faith to know that He who began a good work in us will complete it. (Philippians 1:6) We must know that there is grace for us. Life is an opportunity to get it right. If we have breath in our bodies it points to purpose and all is not lost, we can try again.

"A righteous man falls 7 times, and rises up again"- Proverbs 24:16

Avenge Your Disobedience

Think about the mistakes you have made and help others to not make the same choices. Maybe you can't fix the decisions you have made, but you can help others to learn from them. Take your misery and turn it into your ministry. Teach someone else what not to do because you know the pain of making the wrong decisions. Take that mistake and help someone who is where you once were. Live so you can help teach somebody else how to live. I think the biggest lie is to believe that you are the only one who has failed or made a bad decision.

Jesus tells Peter, "But I have pleaded in prayer for you, Simon, that your faith should not fail. So when you have repented and turned to me again, strengthen your brothers."- Luke 22:32

Jesus foretells Peter falling away and his bad choices but He says when you have repented, help somebody else. Who is being strengthened by your life or story? Receive the grace that God has extended to you by faith and don't allow the devil to continue to torment you with your past. God says if you confess your sins, He is faithful and just enough to forgive you and cleanse you from all unrighteousness. (1John 1:9) If God has forgiven you, forgive yourself.

I've spent too many days beating myself up because I refused to receive God's grace. But I've also felt guilt in such a way that I never wanted to make certain decisions again. The consequences and results were too painful. When I receive God's forgiveness, I receive His grace. It's a prideful thing to not receive grace. In fact, pride prevents us from receiving grace. We focus so much on the sin that we ignore the Savior. We focus so much on the guilt we ignore the grace. We focus so much on the past that we ignore the hope of our faith. Faith over guilt all day. We must confess, "I may have been guilty but I won't live in guilt. I will live in grace. I will live in faith."

Shame

Shame is connected to how one views themselves. According to the dictionary, shame is described as a painful emotion caused by the belief that one is, or is perceived by others to be, inferior or unworthy of affection or respect because of one's actions, thoughts, circumstances, or experiences. Shame doesn't say, "I did something wrong," it says, "something is wrong with me." It connects itself to the identity of a person and allows a person to believe that they are what they have done and experienced. They feel they are unable to change and they are doomed. There is no hope for them. It causes a person to take on the identity of the thing they felt guilty about. They continue the cycle. Never growing or learning from it.

People can make you feel ashamed and do things that bring shame upon you. Abuse causes shame. When a person abuses you it affects the way you view yourself. It's a direct attack against ones identity. Shame produces low self-esteem and a tainted self-image. Tamar was sexually abused in the bible and poured ashes on her head. This signified her disgust of herself. Her shame led to a desolate life. For others it may lead to a destructive life. (2 Samuel 13)

I saw this guy with a tattoo on his forearms and I asked him what it said and he replied, "Hard Head." He said I've been struggling with this all my life. I couldn't grasp why he would tattoo his struggle on himself. His shame had caused him to identify with the very thing he felt guilty about. He felt guilty about being hard headed, being hard headed had led to shame but shame said, "you can't change it, this is who you are." Where he once felt guilty about it, it now became a badge of honor for him.

Shame can also be connected to pride and prevent a person from allowing grace to come in. Those that are shameful cover their sin. Shame doesn't allow you to talk about what you have been through. It will also cause a person not to confess their mistakes and always blame someone else. The person can know their wrong and still blame their reason for being wrong on somebody else. They become defensive when their wrong is pointed out. They don't want to face their wrong because they don't want to face themselves. They are too shameful. They are too shameful to repent so they remorse. Let's look at Judas and Peter in the Bible. Judas betrayed Jesus and filled with shame, he killed himself. Shame leads to self-sabotage. Judas was so ashamed and instead of facing Jesus, he tried to fix it on his own. When his own efforts didn't work, he hung himself. (Matt 27:3-10)

Think about the things in your life you have tried to fix on your own. The things you turned to, to help but made you feel even worse afterwards. Judas never went to Jesus to seek forgiveness and reconciliation. He allowed his conscience and the spirit of shame to beat him up causing him to feel hopeless and leading to suicide. Shame causes people to kill themselves. It's a murderous spirit. It kills. It hinders. It stops you from moving forward and forgiving yourself.

Peter on the other hand denied Christ and when he was exposed, he ran away. But Peter knew how to repent. He didn't lose faith in God's grace. "He was restored and went on to doing the will of God and planting churches." (John 21:15-25)

People who are bound by shame don't take criticism and correction well. Instead of using correction as something to build from, they internalize what is being said and believe it to be truth about who they are. The conversation and comments haunt them long after the discussion is over.

Shame produces avoidance. It causes a person to run from what they have done and experienced instead of facing and overcoming what they are guilty of. Shame has caused decades of secrets in families and bloodlines. It has caused perpetuating cycles in the lives of families and generations. I saw a Facebook post that read, "You repeat what you don't repair." Shame stops a person from moving forward. It's not productive nor does it lead to repentance.

The devil uses our flesh against us, then desires to bind us with guilt and shame to render us ineffective, silence our voices, kill our pursuit of God, and ultimately destroy His will for our lives. But I want to encourage everyone who has made a mistake and fallen, and you're bound by guilt and shame. You feel like God doesn't love you. You feel like He is mad at you and that you have fallen too far from His grace. As long as you're alive there is redemption, there is restoration, there is reconciliation and every day is another opportunity to get it right. God is not like man. He doesn't hold our mistakes over our heads.

When you confess, He is faithful and just

enough to forgive you. Not only does He forgive you, but He will cleanse you from all unrighteousness. (1 John 1:9) Repent. Dust yourself off and get back up. It's not too late. He's waiting to restore you. He has a plan for your life!

Defeat

Guilt and shame, keeps you in a place of defeat. It angers me to see people with so much potential live defeated lives. I mean, they could be so much further along but guilt and shame has robbed them. It has caused them to repeat the very thing they hated. They remain a victim and continue to relive the past instead of creating a better future.

I remember driving and experiencing a bit of frustration. I was traveling and my GPS was not in operation and I missed my turn. And instead of turning around and going the way, I knew. I decided within myself that somehow, I could cross over. That somehow the road I was on was going to take me to my desired destination. After driving for about 15 minutes, I realized that I would have to go back to where I missed the turn and go the way I knew was right. The road I was on was taking me nowhere but in fact it was wasting my time, my gas, and my energy and I was moving further away from where I wanted to be. The problem wasn't the fact that I missed the turn, it was the fact that I didn't turn around!

When we don't face our shame, or mistakes we accept defeat. We hide behind what has happened to us instead of exposing it and killing the behaviors, actions and belief systems that are connected it. The things that has led us in the wrong direction. Faith and humility leads us to a place of repentance and allows us to learn and grow from what we have encountered. Guilt and Shame are not excuses to remain a victim. In fact, you cannot be a victim and a victor at the same time.

God forgives us but we still play a part in the restoration. We must do the work. Sometimes this takes going to the person we have hurt, hearing and understanding their side. Apologizing to them in humility. I think it's important to mention an apology with an excuse is not an apology. Putting faith over failure is found in taking responsibility for your actions, accepting the consequences, forgiving yourself, receiving God's grace and growing from your mistakes.

#Victory

"The present time suffering is not worthy to be compared to the glory that shall be revealed"- Romans 8:18.

"Now thanks be unto God, which always causeth us to triumph in Christ" -2 Corinthians 2:14

Victory is described as an act of defeating an enemy or opponent in a battle, game, or other competition. It's described as success, triumph and win; a successful outcome of a struggle. There is no victory without opposition in the same manner there is no victory outside of Christ. Now unto Him who causes us to triumph. (2 Corinthians 2:14) Victory is Christ. He alone has defeated every enemy, opposition, struggle or pain we will face. And not only has he defeated it, He has given us the power to walk in the victory from it.

"For this purpose, the Son of God was manifested, that he might destroy the works of the devil. -1 John 3:8
Behold, I give unto you power to tread on serpents and scorpions, and over all the power of the enemy..."
-Luke 10:19

    It's our faith that gives us access to power and victory. Our faith is always under attack because it's the gateway to our victory. Jesus spoke about not being able to do miracles in certain areas due to the unbelief of the people. Because the people did not believe the people remained defeated, broken and hurting. In life, we are faced with a lot of obstacles and problems, but the wonderful thing about it is we have the solution, Jesus.

    I once heard an analogy about baking a cake and the ingredients it requires. The eggs, the flour, the butter, none of which are good if eaten by themselves. These ingredients represent the things we face in life, the warfare, the battles, the hurts, the pains the disappointments and the trials. They don't feel or look good. These things come to challenge our faith and are used to build our character. If submitted unto God, can be used these things to bake/ make something wonderful, something beneficial like a cake that you and others can eat of. Only God can take the worst of situations and then use them to make something victorious.

Stubborn Faith

When I think of stubborn faith I think of Shadrach, Meshach and Abednego. I like saying those names! They were known as the three Hebrew boys. They were cliqued up. They were homeboys. Those around them plotted against them because they served God and they were different. They didn't like them so they sought the King to have a royal decree passed. The decrees said that they had to bow to a golden image, a false and idol god. Those around, their haters, wanted to distort their faith. King Nebachnazzer ruled that the individuals that didn't bow would be placed in the fiery furnace. They would be killed if they did not compromise. They were threatened and faced with opposition that might cost them their life. Their response was...

"If it be so, our God whom we serve is able to deliver us from the burning fiery furnace, and he will deliver us out of thine hand, O king. ^{18} But if not, be it known unto thee, O king, that we will not serve thy gods, nor worship the golden image which thou hast set up." - Daniel 3:17

They chose to believe God over their very breath. Their faith was so stubborn, they said even if God does not deliver us, I know He is able and I still will not bow to your gods. Whoa! This is **#IStillBelieve** on max! The king got so mad at their loyalty and faithfulness to God, he turned the heat up seven times greater. He wanted to make sure they were going to fry. Maybe before the king thought, I'll just scare them a little bit, put a little heat on them, a little pressure on them and then they will bow. When they said they will not be moved, the king basically said kill 'em. Turn the heat up!

This is what the enemy does in our lives. He tries to turn the heat up to see if we will compromise, to see if we will disobey God, to see if we will turn back or lose faith. The goal of the enemy is to steal and destroy our faith. When there is no faith in God, anything can rule.

The king ordered for them to be tied and thrown into the furnace. The bible says it was so hot those that threw him in the furnace were killed. Some people will kill themselves trying to take you out... that's another book! When the king looked into the furnace he saw four men instead of three and described the fourth man as looking like the son of God. What I love about God is that He doesn't allow us to face the furnace alone. We don't have to face trials and troubles alone, He is with us. The three Hebrew boys came out the furnace unharmed they had no reside that they had even been in the fire.

God will give you the victory in such a way, no one will even be able to tell you have went through all you have gone through and faced all you have faced. What's even more amazing about this story is, the king and the people around witnessed a miracle. The king was so moved that he said, if anyone even said something about the God they served, they would be punished. He also promoted them. They went from the furnace to the province. He gave them special knowledge, interest and responsibility. Shadrach, Meshach and Abednego experienced victory in a real way. It was their stubborn faith in God that not only blessed them, but those around them were able to see the true and living God they served.

The deepest level of worship is praising God despite pain, thanking God during a trial, trusting him when tempted, surrendering while suffering, and loving him when he seems distant.

Victory lies in our choice to trust God with our lives and putting faith over anything we may face. We must adopt the attitude that going back is not an option! I may stumble going ahead. I may not always get it right. Things may get rough, but at the end of the day, I'm going ahead! Going back is not an option and staying stagnant is not a choice. Faith enables us to make the right decisions despite the opposition we face and emotions we feel. Giving up is not an option because on the other side of our **#IStillBelieve** is **Victory**!

TAMAR

SEXUAL ABUSE SUPPORT GROUP

HEAL THE HURT.
END THE SHAME.
BE VICTORIOUS.

Tamar Sexual Abuse Support Group seeks to empower all those affected by sexual abuse by providing them with proven principles. These principles, along with the application of the participant, will empower an individual to become whole and healthy—spiritually, relationally, and emotionally. Tamar provides a 12-week support group that unveils the many sides of sexual abuse. This group is lead by sexual abuse survivors and compassionate people who have a desire to serve as an instrument of healing and restoration in the lives of those affected by sexual abuse.

BRANCH OUTREACH CENTER

WWW.BRANCHOUTREACH.ORG

References

Chapter 1
Hillsong Worship."Healer".This is Our God. 2008.Cd

Chapter 2
Merriam- Webster Online, s.v "guilt", accessed September 29,2017, http://www.merriam-webster.com/dictionary/guilt
Merriam- Webster Online, s.v "shame", accessed September 29,2017, http://www.merriam-webster.com/dictionary/shame

Chapter 4
Wikipedia. "Fear." The Free Encycolpedia, accessed August 20,2017, http://en.wikipedia.org/wiki/Fear

BibleHub.com, s.v. " yirah", accessed October 2,2017, htt://biblehub.com/greek/794.htm.

Chapter 5
Merriam- Webster Online, s.v "rejection", accessed September 29,2017, http://www.merriam-webster.com/dictionary/rejection

Chapter 6

Wikipedia. "guilt." The Free Encycolpedia, accessed August 20,2017, http://en.wikipedia.org/wiki/guilt

Wikipedia. "shame." The Free Encycolpedia, accessed August 20,2017, http://en.wikipedia.org/wiki/shame

Chapter 7
Merriam- Webster Online, s.v "victory", accessed September 29,2017, http://www.merriam-webster.com/dictionary/victory

ABOUT THE AUTHOR

Asia Thomas is an author and leader. She started a movement called #IStillBelieve challenging and inspiring others not to give up. She involves herself in outreach and being a voice to this generation. She is passionate about Christ and seeing people lives changed for His glory. God has given her a message of faith that will impact the world.

www.ingramcontent.com/pod-product-compliance
Lightning Source LLC
Chambersburg PA
CBHW071231090426
42736CB00014B/3039